anythink

D0602182

Transportation

by Mari Schuh

A 4D BOOK

PEBBLE
a capstone imprint

Download the Capstone 4D app!

- Ask an adult to download the Capstone 4D app.

- Scan the cover and stars inside the book for additional content.

When you scan a spread, you'll find fun extra stuff to go with this book! You can also find these things on the web at www.capstone4D.com using the password: buses.01426

Pebble Books are published by Pebble
1710 Roe Crest Drive,
North Mankato, Minnesota 56003
www.mycapstone.com

Library of Congress Cataloging-in-Publication Data
Names: Schuh, Mari C., 1975- author.
Title: Buses : a 4D book / by Mari Schuh.
Description: North Mankato, Minnesota : Pebble,
a Capstone imprint, [2019] |
  Series: Little pebble. Transportation. | Audience:
  Ages 4–7.
Identifiers: LCCN 2018004151 (print)
LCCN 2018012033 (ebook) | ISBN
9781977101464 (eBook PDF) | ISBN
9781977101426 (hardcover) | ISBN
9781977101440 (pbk.)

Subjects: LCSH: Buses—Juvenile literature.
| CYAC: Buses. | LCGFT: Picture books.
| Instructional and educational works.
Classification: LCC TL232 (ebook) | LCC TL232
.S326 2019 (print) | DDC 629.28/333—dc23
LC record available at https://lccn.loc.
gov/2018004151

Editorial Credits
Karen Aleo, editor; Juliette Peters, designer;
Jo Miller, media researcher; Kris Wilfahrt,
production specialist

Photo Credits
Getty Images: Keith Brofsky, 17; iStockphoto:
kali9, 15; Shutterstock: Art Konovalov, 20–21,
Azami Adiputera, 13, Corepics VOF, 10–11,
Mikbiz, cover, ND700, 19, SHINJONGHO, 9,
Vietnam Stock Images, 5, 7

Design Element
Shutterstock: T.Sumaetho

Table of Contents

At the Bus Stop

People wait for the bus.

Here it comes!

TUYẾN SỐ 47: ĐI BẬT TRÁNG
TUYẾN SỐ 54: ĐI BẮC NINH
TUYẾN SỐ 58: ĐI MÊ LINH
E3.2
TUYẾN SỐ 204: ĐI THUẬN THÀNH

E3.3

XN XE ĐIỆN HÀ NỘI

They safely get on the bus.

Let's go!

Parts

Buses have engines.

Many buses use diesel fuel.

The bus driver starts the engine.

engine

Look at the mirrors.

They help bus drivers

see traffic.

Look at the storage area.

This bus holds luggage.

It's ready to go!

Kinds

A school bus takes kids to school.

It takes them home too.

A city bus follows routes

in the city.

It takes people to work.

An intercity bus goes on

long trips.

It has bathrooms.

Double-decker buses are tall.

They have two floors!

Do you ride a bus?

Glossary

diesel fuel—a heavy oil that burns to make power

engine—a machine that makes the power needed to move something

intercity—traveling between cities

luggage—suitcases and bags people take with them when they travel

route—the road or course followed to get somewhere

storage—a place where things are kept until they are needed

traffic—cars, trucks, and buses that are moving on a road

Read More

Ian, Nicholas. *Riding to School in My Little Yellow School Bus.* On the Move. Minneapolis: Cantata Learning, 2016.

Pettiford, Rebecca. *Bus Drivers.* Community Helpers. Minneapolis: Jump!, 2015.

Reinke, Beth Bence. *School Buses on the Go.* Machines That Go. Minneapolis: Lerner Publications, 2018.

Internet Sites

Use FactHound to find Internet sites related to this book.

Visit *www.facthound.com*

Just type in 9781977101426 and go.

Super-cool stuff!

Check out projects, games and lots more at
www.capstonekids.com

Critical Thinking Questions

1. How do buses help people?

2. How are the different buses the same? How are they different?

3. Why might people use buses instead of other vehicles?

Index